discovermore

*The Lives of Animals*

# How Animals Feed and Hunt



Doug Bradley

Britannica Educational Publishing

IN ASSOCIATION WITH

THE ROSEN PUBLISHING GROUP

Published in 2024 by Britannica Educational Publishing (a trademark of Encyclopædia Britannica, Inc.) in association with The Rosen Publishing Group, Inc.
2544 Clinton Street, Buffalo, NY 14224



Distributed exclusively by Rosen Publishing.
To see additional Britannica Educational Publishing titles, go to rosenpublishing.com.



Editor: Greg Roza
Book Design: Michael Flynn

Photo Credits: Cover Martin Mecnarowski/Shutterstock.com; (series background) Dai Yim/Shutterstock.com; p. 4 Richard Seeley/Shutterstock.com; p. 5 Jaromir Chalabala/Shutterstock.com; p. 6 smereka/Shutterstock.com; p. 7 Linda Marie Caldwell/Shutterstock.com; p. 9 (top) EvaLes/Shutterstock.com; p. 9 (bottom) tonyzhao120/Shutterstock.com; p. 10 Vladimir Kogan Michael/Shutterstock.com; Cathy Keifer/Shutterstock.com; p. 13 Ondrej Prosicky/Shutterstock.com; p. 13 (top) Vitaliy6447/Shutterstock.com; p. 15 Artem Avetisyan/Shutterstock.com; p. 16 Grey Carnation/Shutterstock.com; p. 17 Martin Prochazkacz/Shutterstock.com; p. 18 Calamia/Shutterstock.com; p. 19 Greens and Blues/Shutterstock.com; p. 20 Choksawatdikorn/Shutterstock.com; p. 21 Mcmortgreen/Shutterstock.com; p. 23 (top) Jane Rix/Shutterstock.com; p. 23 slowmotiongli/Shutterstock.com; p. 24 Astrid Gast/Shutterstock.com; p. 25 Cathy Keifer/Shutterstock.com; p. 26 nekomamire/Shutterstock.com; p. 27 Lutsenko_Oleksandr/Shutterstock.com; p. 29 Lewis Burnett/Shutterstock.com.

**Cataloging-in-Publication Data**

Names: Bradley, Doug, 1971-.
Title: How animals feed and hunt / Doug Bradley.
Description: New York : Britannica Educational Publishing, in Association with Rosen Educational Services. 2024. | Series: Discover more: the lives of animals | Includes glossary and index.
Identifiers: ISBN 9781642828726 (library bound) | ISBN 9781642828719 (pbk) | ISBN 9781642828733 (ebook)
Subjects: LCSH: Animals--Food--Juvenile literature. | Predation (Biology)--Juvenile literature.
Classification: LCC QL756.5 B683 2024 | DDC 591.5′3–dc23

Manufactured in the United States of America



CPSIA Compliance Information: Batch #CSBRIT24. For further information contact Rosen Publishing at 1-800-237-9932.

# Contents

# Feeding Time

Animals and plants are both organisms, or living things. All living things need food and water to live. Plants can make their own food, but animals must get their food from their surroundings.

Pets and other animals that are taken care of by humans have food brought to them. Wild animals, though, have to **forage**.

Grizzly bears catch salmon from streams.

Dogs that are kept as pets don't live in the wild, so they beg for food instead of having to hunt for it.

Animals eat either plants or other animals. Some animals eat both. The animals that eat plants are called herbivores. They search for places that have lots of grass or trees, such as fields or forests. Meat eaters, or carnivores, hunt for their meals. They catch and kill other animals to eat.

The way animals eat can be different from animal to animal. Their hunting and feeding styles change based on what, when, and how they eat.

## WORD WISE

**Forage means to find food using senses, such as sight, sound, and smell.**

# An Animal's Diet

Food chains describe what living things eat in the wild. Most living things eat more than one type of animal or plant, so their food chains overlap to form food webs.

Most food chains start with plants. Scientists call plants **producers**. They get energy from the sun. Animals are known as consumers because they consume, or eat, other living things.

Cows feed on plant matter, like grass.

Hyenas are scavengers. A group of them feed on a zebra.

Animals that look for other animals to eat are called predators. Animals that predators track, kill, and eat are known as prey. Most predators like to eat animals that they have killed rather than animals that are already dead.

Scavengers are animals that eat carrion, or the meat of dead animals they usually have not killed themselves. Some types of scavengers eat only carrion. Other animals may eat carrion, but also hunt prey to eat.

## WORD WISE

**Producers make their own food. They are consumed by other organisms for energy.**

# Truth Behind a Tooth

Carnivorous animals have sharp teeth that can tear and chew meat. Most also have claws that let them catch and hold their prey. Any animal—including insects—is possible food for a carnivore. Moles and many kinds of birds eat insects. Even some insects, such as praying mantises, eat other insects.

Plant-eating animals often have broad, flat teeth that are useful for chewing and grinding plants. These animals include horses, sheep, rabbits, and elephants. Some birds and plenty of insects are plant eaters as well. Animals that eat plants often become a carnivore's meal.

Some animals are omnivores, meaning they eat both meat and plants. Omnivores, such as people, have teeth that can cut and tear, but also teeth that can grind.

A wolf uses its many sharp teeth for catching and killing prey.

## compare and contrast

Carnivores depend on other animals for their meals, but herbivores depend on plants. How might the ways these two groups find and eat food be the same or different?

A giraffe's long neck helps it to reach tree leaves.

# Finding Food

Animals that live in the wild must search for their own food. Herbivores, such as zebras and giraffes, live near places that have lots of grasses and trees they can eat. Many animals move from one place to another at certain times of the year. This process is called migration. Migration can make it easier for animals to find food.

A hawk swoops down to catch a fish.

A grasshopper is caught in the sticky strands of a spider web.

Carnivores get food by hunting. Some hunt during the day, while others sleep during the day and hunt at night. Some find and kill prey alone. Others hunt in groups, known as packs. Chasing and catching food is one way that carnivores hunt. Some animals ambush their prey. This means they hide and wait for prey to come to them. Spiders build webs that allow them to trap their prey.

## Consider This

Many animals migrate to search for food. What are some other reasons an animal might migrate?

# Different Species

Similar groups of animals often have similar feeding and hunting behaviors. To better understand these habits, it helps to know the different groups.

A vertebrate is an animal with a backbone. Mammals (including humans), birds, fish, reptiles, and amphibians are all vertebrates.

Mammals are animals that breathe air and grow hair. Most mammals live on land, although some live on land and in the water. There are about 5,000 species, or kinds, of living mammals. Human beings are mammals.

Birds are the only living animals with feathers. While all have wings, not all can fly. There are more than 9,000 species of birds alive today.

Fish are animals that live in water. There are more than 30,000 species of fish. New species of fish are discovered every year!

Some mammals live in water all of the time, such as dolphins and whales.

## compare and contrast

Monkeys and humans are both primates, meaning they have similar body structures. What are some differences between the two primates? What are some similarities?

Can you name this type of bird?

Reptiles are air-breathing, cold-blooded animals that are covered in scales rather than hair or fur. Most have four limbs, except for snakes, which have none. Today, there are about 6,000 known species of reptiles.

Amphibians can live on land or in water. There are three main groups of amphibians: frogs and toads, salamanders, and wormlike creatures called caecilians. Altogether, there are more than 6,500 species of amphibians.

Invertebrates are animals without backbones. Many invertebrates have soft bodies. Some are unprotected, but others have shells or tough skin. Some invertebrates—such as spiders, insects, and crabs—have an exoskeleton. These animals are called arthropods, meaning they have a skeleton-like covering outside their body.

## Consider This

Dinosaurs were reptiles that became **extinct** 65 million years ago. What do you think they fed on? How do you think they foraged for their meals?

The disks on a tree frog's fingers and toes help them to climb.

## WORD WISE

**Extinct means to completely die out and have no more living members of your group on Earth.**

# Mammals

Mammals can be carnivores, omnivores, or herbivores. All female mammals have glands that can produce milk to feed their babies. Many carnivorous parents also kill prey and bring it to their young. The young are fed this way until they are old enough to get their own food.

Young mammals learn many kinds of **behavior**, including how to hunt and find food. They learn by watching what their parents and other older animals do.

Mammals produce milk for their babies, such as the mother cat feeding her kittens.

A lioness will teach her cubs to hunt, meaning it is a learned behavior.

Practicing hunting skills is important. Sometimes adult cats—from house cats to lions and cheetahs—give prey that is alive but hurt to their young so that they can practice catching and killing food.

Once they are grown, carnivorous mammals may hunt in groups or alone. When plant-eating mammals live and eat in groups, they can better protect themselves from danger.

## WORD WISE

**Behavior is the way a living thing acts.**

# Birds

Birds often feed on seeds, nuts, and fruit. Many also eat insects. Birds of prey catch and eat animals, including other birds. These birds are usually large and strong. Their good eyesight helps them see prey from far away.

Hummingbirds have forked tongues to sip sweet nectar from flowers.

Sandpipers use their beaks to poke into the sand on a beach to gather food. Their name makes sense!

Birds have beaks instead of a jaw with teeth (although a few birds, such as ducks, do have serrated beaks). Long beaks are good for digging in the sand or sticking into holes in trees to find food. Sharp beaks are good at tearing food into bite-sized pieces. Birds of prey also usually have sharp claws that are useful for holding and killing prey.

Most carnivorous birds like to catch live food. However, some of them, such as vultures, feed on carrion and garbage because they are scavengers.

## Consider This

Owls and vultures are birds of prey. Can you think of any others?

# Fish

Smaller fish are often preyed on by other, larger fish. Some fish search for food using "feelers" around their mouths. Others simply open their mouths and catch prey while they swim. Still others hide, catching smaller fish that swim too close.

The smallest fish eat tiny water plants and animals called plankton. Plankton can be scraped off of rocks or simply eaten as they float in the water. Plenty of fish eat plankton using their mouths, but some pull in plankton through their **gills**.

Plankton use energy from the sun to help them breathe.

This fish has caught a smaller one for dinner!

Most fish swallow their food whole. Fish teeth are used mainly to catch prey or to collect plant foods, not to chew. They can be in a fish's jaw, in their mouth bones, and even inside their throat, near the gills.

## WORD WISE

**Gills let fish breathe underwater. They are similar to a mammal's lungs.**

# Reptiles

Many reptiles are carnivores that eat all kinds of animals, including insects, birds, frogs, mice, and fish. Many reptiles catch live food, but some will eat carrion. A few members of the reptile family, including some lizards and a type of land turtle called a tortoise, eat only plants. (Other turtles usually eat things such as worms, snails, and insects.)

In general, the smaller the reptile, the smaller its prey. Very large snakes can eat mammals such as small pigs and deer. Some types of crocodiles have been known to attack and eat humans. However, crocodiles don't eat humans as much as they eat small mammals, birds, and even other crocodiles.

A tortoise snacks on strawberries.

## compare and contrast

Turtles eat meat, but tortoises eat plants. How do you think their behaviors when searching for food are different?

Snakes eat their prey whole.

# Amphibians

Amphibians have a wide variety of foods in their diet. Frog and toad eggs hatch into tadpoles, which are more like fish than frogs. Because they have small mouths, tadpoles eat tiny living things that grow on water plants.

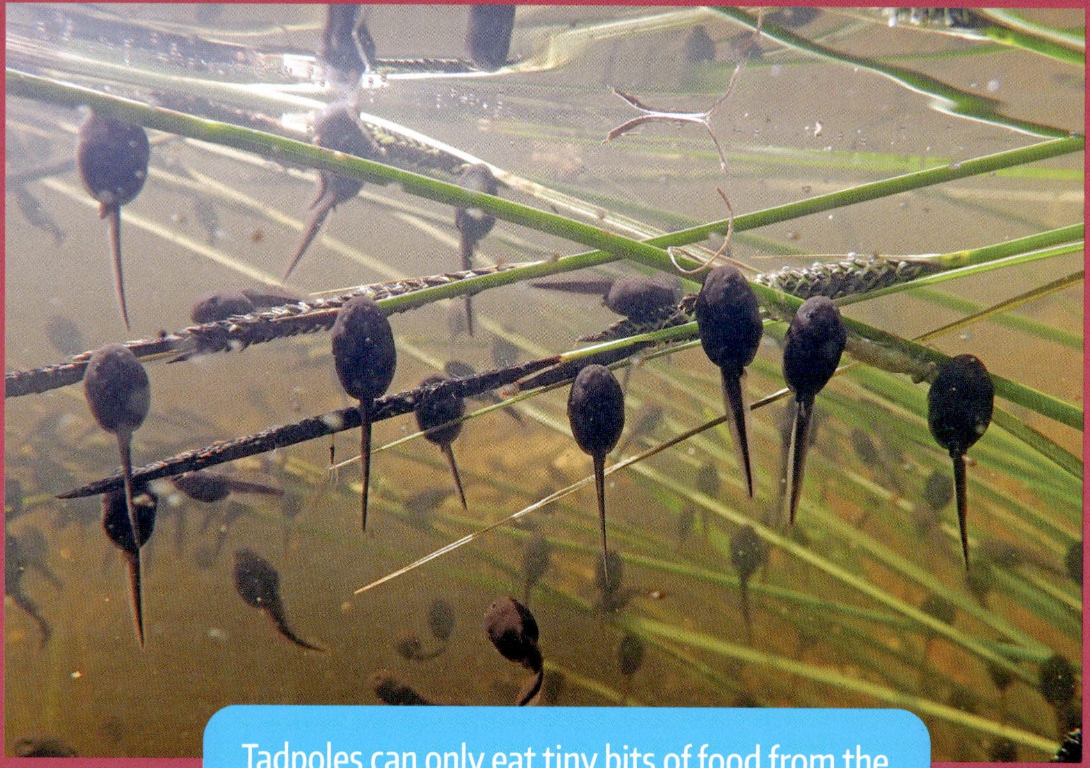

Tadpoles can only eat tiny bits of food from the water because of their small size.

Frogs can snatch their prey by **flicking** their tongue.

Adult frogs and toads mainly eat small boneless animals such as insects, worms, and spiders. Some large adult salamanders and frogs even eat small birds and mammals. Some salamanders eat other salamanders. Salamanders that look for food in the water simply suck prey into their mouths. Caecilians eat worms.

Toads and frogs catch food by flicking out their long, sticky tongues and swallowing prey whole. Land salamanders use their tongues to help capture prey, too, as they can flick it in the blink of an eye!

## WORD WISE

**Flicking means to move fast and swiftly.**

# Invertebrates

The biggest group of invertebrates are insects. In fact, insects are the largest group of animals. Plants, animals, and other living things make a nice meal for insects. Certain insects, such as fleas, suck blood from other animals.

Invertebrates that live in water may eat algae. Some, such as squid, catch and eat other water animals. Invertebrates that live on land, such as snails, eat plants, carrion, and other invertebrates.

A squid will use its tentacles to catch prey.

A praying mantis has small spikes in its legs that can be used to catch prey, such as moths.

Many carnivorous arthropods have special body parts near their mouths that help them gather food. Some arthropods use poison, given by a bite or sting, to attack prey. The prey is then easier to catch and eat because the poison hurts or kills it.

## Consider This

Invertebrates use their special skills to catch food. Can you think of any other animals that use special skills to catch food?

# Eating Instincts

Diet and foraging behaviors are very different from animal to animal. Elephants push down young trees to feed on the roots, twigs, and leaves. Sharks use smell to track down other sea animals, circling their prey before attacking from below. A group of scavenging hyenas may drive off a small group of lions and steal their kill.

From very good eyesight or hearing to sharp claws and steel-trap jaws, carnivores are made to hunt. Herbivores, meanwhile, have special teeth and even extra stomachs to help them feed on plants. The way an animal is built best helps it to search for and consume the food it needs to survive.

**compare and contrast**

What are some other differences between meat-eating and plant-eating animals, besides their diets? What are some similarities?

Sharks swim around prey in a circle, before attacking with their sharp teeth!

# Glossary

**algae** A group of living things that, like plants, make their own food but are different from plants in other ways.

**arthropod** An animal that does not have a backbone but does have shell-like coverings or exoskeletons. Spiders, butterflies, and crabs are all arthropods.

**carrion** Dead animal matter.

**exoskeleton** A hard covering outside an animal's body.

**food chain** The order in which living things use other living things for food. For example: sun, grass, mouse, owl.

**gland** A part of an animal's body that produces substances to help the body function.

**invertebrate** An animal without a backbone.

**nectar** A sugary liquid made by plants.

**predator** An animal that hunts and kills other animals for food.

**prey** An animal hunted or killed by another animal for food.

**salamanders** Animals that look like lizards but have smooth skin instead of scales.

**scales** Small, flat plates that cover the bodies of many reptiles.

**scavenger** A living thing that eats carrion or garbage.

**serrated** Having sharp notches, much like the blade of a saw.

**tadpole** The young, early-stage form of frogs or toads.

**tortoise** A turtle that lives on the land.

**track** To find and follow closely.

# For More Information

## Books

Sweet, Paul. *The Fantastic World of Birds of Prey*. San Diego, CA: Puppy Dogs & Ice Cream, 2022.

Tyrrell, Nichola. *Foxton Primary Science: Carnivores, Herbivores and Omnivores.* London, UK: Foxton Books, 2019.

Wilsdon, Christina. *Ultimate Predatorpedia: The Most Complete Predator Reference Ever*. Washington, D.C.: National Geographic Kids, 2018.

## Websites

**A to Z Animals**
*a-z-animals.com*
This website offers detailed information on Earth's many varied species of animals.

**National Geographic**
*nationalgeographic.com*
This website provides updated information and stories about the natural and historical elements of the world, including animals.

Publisher's note to educators and parents: Our editors have carefully reviewed these websites to ensure that they are suitable for students. Many websites change frequently, however, and we cannot guarantee that a site's future contents will continue to meet our high standards of quality and educational value. Be advised that students should be closely supervised whenever they access the internet.

# Index